Building the Perfect Page for SEO

Building the Perfect Page for SEO

Table of Contents

Introduction

First off, I want to welcome you and Thank you for purchasing my book. I have been in SEO for many years and hope that sharing my knowledge here about on-page SEO will help you rank better in search engines. There are so many different opinions of SEO these days that it's difficult to understand what you will actually need to do in order to get your site ranked. The level of misinformation tends to outweigh the really good SEO advice that is based on time tested, penalty proof methods that continue to work. The advice I offer in this book is based on my knowledge of building webpages and case studies that I have performed on different sites to determine the best methods available.

So without further ado, let's jump right into the Building the Perfect Page for SEO guide.

Building the Perfect Page

Building the perfect page on your website is not as difficult as you might think. In this book I will give you advice on each different part of the page and how it should be structured to get the maximum SEO benefit.

The very first thing you'll need to determine when adding a page to your website is the subject or keyword phrase you will be targeting. It's important to first determine this in order to ensure that all elements of the page are focused on this subject. For instance, if your page was about 'dog training' you wouldn't want to include 'cat training' information. Instead make sure that one page is focused more on a single subject. Vary from the subject is okay as long as it pertains to the main subject.

A great way to branch away from the main subject is by using related keywords (also known as LSI keywords). However, you'll need to include a variety of related keywords that are still focused on the main subject. Consider your page is about 'wooden widgets' you can actually break down that subject by using 'green wooden widgets' or 'widgets made of wood'. This can help you in different ways.

The first being that the keyword isn't stuffed in the content that you're writing and the second is it gives the content on the page more focus. These related keywords also eliminate any penalties that search engines sometimes impose for keyword stuffing when you use the keyword you're targeting too many times in your content.

So now that you've got the main concept and keyword phrase you want to build upon you can start building the page from there. The following topics are the most important for on page SEO. Each topic is broken down in a separate chapter to better explain how to craft each element. It's important to attempt to make sure each point is adhered to for best results.

URL

Each page on your website is located on its own URL. It's the bit in the address bar on your browser that allows users to find your page and search engines to point searchers at your page when they search for a related query. The URL of your page counts towards your overall SEO score and helps search engines determine what your page is about.

Your URL should ideally be less than 100 characters including your domain name. Longer URLs are okay however the best results are less than 100 characters. It should also not contain any 'stop' words such as the, is, or, etc.

It's also best to place your post in a category that is displayed in the URL. This is also known as silo structure. For instance, let's say you have a category for 'Widgets' on your site. And the URL was:

YourSite.com/widgets/

Now if you add a new post into that category your URL should look like this:

YourSite.com/widgets/redwidgets.htm

This helps your site in terms of SEO by telling search engines that your site is silo structured and that the 'redwidgets.htm' page is in a larger category about widgets. It can give much more link power since it's considered in a related category to its main subject.

You can even drill down further for child categories if they are on your site with a URL structure like this:

YourSite.com/widgets/wooden/redwidgets.html

This would mean the widgets are in the wooden category and they are also 'red widgets' by using this structure.

When the URL is displayed in search engines it is displayed with the categories as a clickable link in search results on Google. If a user is searching for blue widgets and your red widgets page is shown in search results they are able to click on the Widgets category of your site which can lead to a new visitor.

It's also a good idea to have URLs that doesn't have punctuation marks and long numbers. If you can add your keyword or related keyword to the URL in both the page URL and the category URL then your URL would be optimized properly.

To Breakdown:

- Your URL needs to contain your keyword less any stop words

- Your URL should contain a category that the post is in and related to

- Your URL should be less than 100 characters total including any categories and file extensions

- Your URL should not contain any punctuation marks or long strings of text or numbers

Title

The title of your page is one of the most important parts of your page. It plays vital roles in how your page is ranked and how users see your page and react to it. When searching the title is the very first thing searchers will notice about your site. So it's important to attempt to 'close the click' from just the title alone.

This means that the title needs to be a call to action. The title should entice the user to click on your site link in order to find the solution to the problem they are searching for. It is also best to include your keyword phrase in the title and keep the keyword phrase close to the beginning of the title.

A great way to look at call to action title is to look at some of the ad copy that is displayed in search results for ideas. Although your site may be informative it still needs to attract clicks from search results.

Search engines may use the information related to click through rate on your url to determine ranking your site. Consider this: A user is displayed 10 results yet the result in the 4th place gets more clicks per impression than any of the other results. This would mean that the site in 4th place may be more connected with what the user is searching for. Take this into account and the site should move up in rankings.

A good way to determine CTR (Click Through Rate) is by using Google's Webmaster Tools. It lists popular searches for your site and also what your current CTR is for each keyword phrase. Tweaking your title to get the best CTR possible is best.

The length of the title will vary but it needs to be a minimum of 40 characters. Keep in mind longer titles over 60 characters may have the end removed and replaced with '…'. If you must use a longer title make sure the keyword phrase is located in the first 56 characters.

The title will also need to be unique on each page on your site that you wish to rank for. Many website owners will make a title that is the same on each page of their site however this is extremely bad for SEO.

Title Breakdown:

-Minimum of 40 characters

-Title must be a call to action

-Title must contain keyword phrase and if possible closer to the beginning of the title

-The title must be unique on any page of your site that you wish to rank in search results

Description (meta description)

The meta description, like the title, is displayed in search results which are shown to users who search for your keyword phrase. By manipulating the title and meta description of your page you effectively write ad copy that is displayed in search results. You can also match the title and description to work together in some cases.

The meta description needs to contain the keyword phrase you are targeting and it also needs to be near the beginning. However, the importance of having a better call to action will supersede the need to have the keyword close to the beginning. It's more important to get a better CTR than to have the keyword closer to the beginning.

Like the title your meta description will need to be unique on all pages that you wish to rank for in search engines. If you do not specify a meta description search engines will pull text from your page in order to display in search results. The problem is they may decide to display information that doesn't entice the user to click causing the CTR to decline.

The length of the meta description needs to be 120 to 156 characters total. Descriptions less than 120 characters may not be displayed and could be replaced by text on your page. You can also end the meta description mid-sentence if need be to draw more clicks.

One key thing to remember when crafting a title and meta description for your page is to get the user to click on the link. It's important to realize you're not attempting to sell anything or promote anything to the user instead you're only trying to get the click, not the sale.

Meta Description Breakdown:

-Meta Description should be between 120 characters and 156 characters

-Meta description needs to contain the keyword phrase preferably near the beginning of the description

-All your meta descriptions need to be unique on each page of your site.

Other Meta Tags

There are many other meta tags that you can use in your website. However, the meta description is the most important.

A tag that is obsolete now is promoted heavily on many SEO sites and it's the meta keywords tag. Since the meta keywords tag was abused heavily abused years ago it almost completely ignored now by search engines.

Although it may not help you however it could hurt your rankings. Websites would stuff the meta keywords tags with hundreds or sometimes thousands of keywords to help their sites rank. Once search engines caught on to this they put in algorithms to penalize sites that stuffed this tag with keywords. Although it may not help your site, if you stuff the keywords tag it could hurt your rankings.

Some lesser known search engines may index your site and use these meta keywords that you supply. However, don't expect much traffic from these sites. The risk versus reward typically is not worth it for the scarce amount of traffic you get.

Other Meta Tags Breakdown:

-It's best not to use this tag

-If you use the meta keywords tag then only supply 3 to 5 keyword phrases

Headings

Pages are built using a hierarchy structure. First the title, then the headings on the page need to be addressed. This includes headings all the way to heading six. Each of these headings on the page needs to correspond with the page subject or keyword phrase.

Your page should only have a single heading and it should contain your keyword phrase you are targeting. It should also be longer than 40 characters and displayed within the first two paragraphs of the page. Usually, this is accomplished by displaying a summary of the article and then start the article with a heading 1 or H1 tag. A page needs to contain only one H1 tag or heading 1 per page.

Further down the page you'll want to include other heading tags that summarize each bit of content they are connected to. It's also best to include LSI or related keywords in other headings of your post. All the headings that are displayed need to directly relate to the main subject of the page.

Headings Breakdown:

-Each page should only contain one H1 or heading 1 tag and it should contain your keyword phrase

-Other headings on the page need to contain related keyword phrases

-The headings need to directly relate to the content they are summarizing.

Images

Images can add lots of extra influence on a webpage. Many people overlook how important images are when it comes to SEO but they are vital to getting your site noticed not only in the web search portions of Google but also in the image search. Gaining organic traffic from image searches can add a nice addition to your organic traffic.

There are two attributes that all the images on your page must have and those are alt and title. The alt and title needs to contain the keyword phrase you are targeting on the first image. However, any additional images added to the page need to contain related keywords for the alt and title attributes.

One thing you'll need to keep in mind also is the subject matter of your images. They need to be related to your keyword phrase that you are targeting. For instance, even if you decide to use the alt and title of "wooden toys" and use a picture of the London Bridge then it will not help your users nor will it add any credibility to the content.

Although search engines may not use all the information that is contained in some images including descriptions, keywords, and author it's best to place these values in your images if they belong to you. You can do so with an image editing program such as Adobe Photoshop or Gimp.

Images Breakdown:

-Always use keywords and related keywords in alt and title attributes of images

-Only use related images that correspond to the article's subject matter.

Lists and Block Quotes

Lists are a great way to display data that summarizes key points in an article. They work extremely well for Table of Contents and they can also contain keyword phrases related to your main subject.

Block quotes are another area that can be used to summarize content. Make sure if you use block quotes that your keyword phrase or related keyword phrase is contained in the block quote.

Content

Content is what most people on search engines are looking for so when you determine what your page is about with keyword phrases and subject your entire content will need to focus on that subject. Your keyword phrases and related keyword phrases need to be spread throughout your content.

Adding your keyword phrase too many times in an article will likely bring decreased rankings. This is referred to as keyword density and should never exceed 2 % of the total content on your page. Ideally, you should only use a keyword density of around 1% but it must not take the place of quality. Many website owners tend to write for search engine spiders and target a specific number on keyword density. However, this can lead to poor content and machine like readability. It's best to write content for your users and provide valuable content rather than stuffing keywords into the content.

Your content will also need to be at a minimum of 1000 words for each page you are attempting to get ranked. If you want to use more than 1,500 words on a single page you can use pagination tags to connect them so search engines will know that pages are together and should be displayed as such. Having lots of pages with thin content can lead to a penalty from search engines.

It's also important that all of the content on your site is unique and not available or copied anywhere else. A great way to keep an eye on pages of your site is to use plagiarism checkers such as Copyscape.com . Having too much duplicate content can cause your website and all the pages to disappear from search engines so be sure to only post unique content.

Be sure to include things like bolded words, italized words, etc., when building your content. Remember you want to give the users what they are searching for not a bunch of words on a page that contain the keywords you're searching for. By also giving them better content you can improve the bounce rate for your site too.

Having a lower bounce rate on your site means that when a user visits your site they stay on your site and click other links and read content which is good for your site. When a user finds your site in search and then immediately returns to the search results your bounce rate will be really high. This tells search engines that your site wasn't what the user wanted and they will decrease your rankings when your site has a higher bounce rate. There is no set in stone bounce rate because it varies depending on the niche your site is in. However, always strive for a lower bounce rate.

Content Breakdown:

-Content on a page should be a minimum of 1,000 words

-All content must be unique and not available anywhere else online

-Write content for users and not search engines. This can improve bounce rate for your site

Other Elements

There are other elements that you'll want to address on your site that can help your SEO efforts. The first would be bounce rate which was explained in the previous section. Keeping a lower bounce rate can help your site outrank other sites in your niche.

Another element you'll want to include in your site is social signals. Your site needs to include easy ways for users to share and comment on your post. This can help you by giving you social signals once a user shares it. It also helps you gain backlinks to your post when they post to their pages or timelines.

Adding other types of media can also help your page. A related video tends to help a page rank well. Coupled with related images with proper attributes set and your page should be well rounded and full of information.

Other Elements Breakdown:

-Add social buttons to help social signals to your site and encourage sharing

-Add other types of related media including videos related to your keyword phrase

Page Design

There are many things that can both help and hurt your site in terms of SEO. One of the most popular content management systems today is called Wordpress and there are loads of themes that users can install on their Wordpress sites. Many webmasters don't realize however that some of these themes or templates could harm their SEO.

The theme or template of your website should be fast loading. This means that the images, buttons, or javascript needs to be minimal to ensure the page is loaded fast. Slow page load times can harm your rankings. Make sure you optimize images which is usually a huge problem.

Another area of concern is the footer links that are sometimes added to free templates or themes. Make sure if you use these themes or templates that the links are no-follow or removed completely. You may need to purchase the theme to remove the links so be sure to check with the theme details for more information.

The page design should also available on any platform including mobile. Having a site that can handle requests for smaller screens and optimized for mobile will play a larger role in coming updates.

Page Design Breakdown:

-Ensure your page load time is okay by optimizing images, css, and javascript

-Check for unwanted, unrelated links in the footer if you use free themes or templates

-Make your site available in all formats and have a responsive design

Links

Your content will sometimes need to link to other sites online. Sometimes sites that link to other sites can draw a penalty for paid links simply because they don't allow do-follow links as paid links. Because of this it's best to always add the 'rel="nofollow"' attribute to your links. This can also help your site retain more link pagerank as well.

It's best to also link to other pages on your site especially when it's in the same category. This gives the page you link to more importance and also gives your user more information.

You'll also need to link to the category that the page is contained in as well. This linking structure tends to work best and can help boost all the pages that are contained in that category.

It's also best to have less than 12 links that leave your page. Remember as well that with each link you are giving the user an opportunity to leave your site. Having a large amount of links that leave your site could bring a penalty to your site so avoid having more than 12 external links on each page.

Final Thoughts

To really get to the heart of SEO it's important to be able to understand what search engines are searching for themselves. It's the search engine's job to show the best related results to the user who is searching. Take a good look at your site and ask yourself the tough question of is that the site you would want to see if you searched for a particular keyword.

It's important to know that your content and page needs to focus on a single subject and needs to be in the user's interest. If you do this chances are your site will thrive in search results and keep gaining rankings as it gets more and more popular.

Now that you know the type of content that search engines love make sure you continually add more content to your site. Sites that are updated frequently are considered up to date and indexed much faster.

Conclusion

Thank you again for downloading this book!

I hope you enjoyed reading Building the Perfect Page for SEO.

Finally, if you enjoyed this book, please take the time to share your thoughts and **post a review on Amazon**. It'd be greatly appreciated!

Thank you!

Next Steps

-   Write me an honest review about the book – I truly value your opinion and thoughts and I will incorporate them into my next book, which is already underway.

Thank You!